THE HAWTHORN

Sensational
COCKTAILS
& PARTY DRINKS

A collection of classic cocktails and long
cool mixed drinks, perfect to enjoy any time,
bringing a sense of occasion to any
celebration.

MURDOCH BOOKS
Sydney • London

COCKTAILS & PARTY DRINKS

Cocktails are certainly making a comeback. They are popular amongst not only the young and fashionable set but also the more mature and sophisticated.

As a host you do not need a large array of spirits and mixers to entertain. Simply choose two or three cocktails to serve and deliver these with skill and ease. We give you recipes for the most popular cocktails and mixed drinks. We have also included a selection of delicious punches. All the recipes serve one, unless otherwise stated, with suggestions for garnishes and the glassware needed.

When preparing your cocktails, plan ahead. Have a good supply of clean glasses, ice, mixers and garnishes available and serve your cocktails as soon as they are made. Experiment; these recipes can be used as a guide. Above all, enjoy making and creating cocktails.

Cocktail Making

There are only a few techniques to master in cocktail making.
Shake: you will need to fill your cocktail shaker half-full with ice, pour over your ingredients and shake well to mix. The contents are then poured through a strainer into the serving glass.
Stir: ice is added to a mixing glass, the ingredients are poured over the ice and stirred to mix with a long-handled spoon.
Build: this method is used when a drink is made in the serving glass. Fruit juice, cream or soft drink is added and the drink is served with a straw and swizzle stick.

Basic Stock

The basic stock needed to start a cocktail bar would include a good quality brandy, whisky, gin, vodka, light rum, dry and sweet vermouth and others such as Cointreau, Kahlua, Baileys Irish Cream, Galliano and crème de cacao.

You will need a range of mixers like orange juice, lemonade, mineral water and tomato juice. Don't forget to include cream, coconut cream, Angostura Bitters and grenadine.
Garnishes are also important so have citrus fruits, olives, maraschino cherries, salt, sugar, and egg whites.
Some recipes may call for sugar syrup: simply combine 1 cup of white crystal sugar with 1 cup water in a small pan. Bring to the boil. Simmer, stirring until sugar is dissolved. Store the sugar syrup in a bottle in the refrigerator.

ESSENTIAL EQUIPMENT

There are only a few pieces of equipment essential for cocktail making. Many of the basic pieces can be found in your own kitchen.
You will need:

Cocktail shaker: consists of two pieces or cones which overlap when fitted together. To use a shaker, add ice until half full and pour over liquids. Secure the second cone over the first and shake vigorously to mix the cocktail. Strain immediately into serving glass.

Strainer: the traditional strainer is called a Hawthorn strainer. It is stainless steel with a flat base with holes and has an edge of rolled wire to prevent any spillage.

Mixing glass: is used to stir cocktails in and has a pouring lip. You can use a glass jug for this.

Measure: we have used the standard double measure. One side measures out 30 mL and the other side 15 mL. Measures can also be called jiggers, tots or pourers.

Long-handled spoon: this is used to stir cocktails.

Other useful pieces of equipment would include: juice extractor, tongs, teaspoons, chopping board and knife, corkscrew, mallet and can opener. Don't forget clean cloths, cocktail sticks, swizzle sticks and straws.

GLASSES

You do not need a vast array of glassware to present fine cocktails; a few good examples will meet most needs. Always use glass and never serve your cocktails in coloured glasses as they detract from your drink. Glassware should be clean and free from detergents. A hint when washing and drying glasses is to wash, rinse and dry with a clean tea towel, then polish with a fresh tea towel. If possible chill your glasses before use in the refrigerator or fill them with ice while you prepare the cocktail.

These glasses will cover most possibilities when making cocktails.

Cocktail or Martini glass: V-shaped with a long stem to keep the drink cool. It is used for short strong drinks.

Champagne flute: for sparkling drinks and champagne cocktails.

The older style champagne saucer is now used mostly for creamy cocktails.

Large goblet: these glasses vary in size and shape. They can be used for fruity, tropical drinks that are served with lots of ice.

Old-Fashioned tumbler: a short straight-sided glass that is used to serve mixed drinks, short unstrained cocktails and fruit juices.

Highball glass: a tall straight-sided glass used to serve long cool mixed drinks and cocktails.

Brandy balloon: to serve brandy so one can enjoy its heady aroma. Cocktails can also look sensational in these.

Liqueur Coffee glass: to serve special liqueur coffees and Egg Nog.

Other useful glasses would be wine, liqueur and sherry glasses.

WHISKY SOUR

This cocktail is a refreshing pre-dinner drink. Bourbon may replace
whisky, making a Bourbon Sour. You will need sugar syrup for this
recipe (see page 3).
Whisky Sour is best served in an Old-Fashioned tumbler.

ice
45 mL Scotch whisky
30 mL lemon juice
15 mL sugar syrup
lemon peel

1 Shake ice, whisky, lemon juice and sugar syrup in a shaker.
2 Strain into glass over ice. Decorate with a twist of lemon peel.

RUSTY NAIL

A Rusty Nail is one of the best nightcaps you can enjoy.
Our recipe uses equal quantities of Scotch whisky and Drambuie.
You may prefer to increase the whisky by a half measure for
a stronger nightcap.
Serve the Rusty Nail in an Old-Fashioned tumbler.

45 mL Scotch whisky
45 mL Drambuie
ice
lemon twist

Pour the whisky and then the Drambuie over ice in the serving glass.
Add the lemon twist.

OLD-FASHIONED WHISKY

This classic mixed drink is a stimulating afternoon drink
Scotch or Canadian whisky or bourbon may be used.
Serve this drink in an Old-Fashioned tumbler.

1 sugar cube
Angostura Bitters
soda water
ice
60 mL whisky
orange twist
lemon twist

1 Soak the sugar cube in a dash of bitters. Place the sugar cube
in the serving glass and top with a good dash of soda water. Add ice
and stir to dissolve sugar cube.
2 Add whisky, garnish with orange and lemon twist. Serve with
a swizzle stick.

MANHATTAN

Here is a delightful pre-dinner cocktail which can be either dry or sweet depending on whether you use dry or sweet vermouth. A dry Manhattan is garnished with an olive and lemon peel, and a sweet Manhattan is garnished with a maraschino cherry and lemon peel. Canadian or rye whisky is traditionally used.
Serve this drink in a cocktail or Martini glass.

ice cubes
45 mL Canadian whisky
20 mL dry vermouth
Angostura Bitters
1 green olive
knot of lemon peel

1 Stir ice, whisky, vermouth and bitters in a mixing glass.
2 Strain into a Martini glass and garnish with an olive and lemon peel.

WHISKY COBBLER

This potent cocktail can be served as a pre- or after-dinner drink.
Scotch whisky is traditionally used and is topped with a dash
of brandy and curaçao. A dash is the quantity released from
a quick spurt from the bottle.
Serve this drink in a large goblet.

ice
60 mL Scotch whisky
4 dashes of brandy
4 dashes of curaçao
orange twist
pineapple
mint

1 Fill the goblet with ice cubes. Pour over whisky, brandy
and curaçao; stir.
2 Garnish with orange, pineapple and mint; serve with a straw.

MARTINI

Martinis are the perfect pre-dinner cocktails and should always be stirred, not shaken. For a drier Martini use less vermouth. Serve in the classic Martini or cocktail glass.

ice
75 mL gin
15 mL dry vermouth
olive
knot of lemon peel

1 Place ice, gin and vermouth in a mixing glass and stir gently to mix.
2 Strain into a Martini glass and garnish with an olive and lemon peel.

GIMLET

Gimlets are popular as pre-dinner drinks. Use good quality lime
cordial and serve with a good dash of soda (or more if preferred).
Serve in an Old-Fashioned tumbler.

ice
45 mL gin
15 mL lime cordial
soda water
lemon twist

Place ice in serving glass; pour over gin and lime cordial and add a good
dash of soda water. Add lemon; serve with a swizzle stick.

NEGRONI

Negroni are becoming increasingly popular as delicious afternoon or evening drinks. Soda water may be used to lighten the cocktail. Serve Negroni in a cocktail glass or, for a longer drink with soda water, in a highball glass.

ice
30 mL gin
30 mL sweet vermouth
30 mL Campari
soda water
orange twist

1 Place ice, gin, vermouth and Campari in mixing glass; stir to combine.
2 Strain into a cocktail glass. Add a dash of soda water and garnish with orange twist.

WHITE LADY

This enticing drink is perfect to sip as a pre-dinner cocktail. You will need a dash of beaten egg white; take care to shake it well. A White Lady is best served in a cocktail glass. Try sugar-frosting your glass with grenadine sugar (see page 60).

ice
30 mL gin
15 mL Cointreau
15 mL lemon juice
dash egg white

1 Place ice, gin, Cointreau, lemon juice and egg white in a shaker; shake well.
2 Strain into serving glass.

GIN SLING

This classic cocktail is a refreshing pre-dinner drink. You can use whisky or brandy in place of gin.
Serve your Gin Sling in a highball glass.

ice
45 mL gin
30 mL lemon juice
dash grenadine
soda water
lemon twist
maraschino cherry

Place ice in serving glass. Add gin, lemon juice and grenadine and top with soda water. Garnish with lemon twist and a cherry; serve with a swizzle stick.

FALLEN ANGEL

There are two versions of this cocktail, each quite different
We give you our favourite.
Serve this version in a cocktail glass.

ice
45 mL gin
15 mL green crème de menthe
30 mL lemon juice
dash Angostura Bitters
maraschino cherry

1 Place ice, gin, crème de menthe, lemon juice and bitters in a shaker.
Shake well to mix.
2 Strain into a cocktail glass and garnish with a cherry.

SCREWDRIVER

This ever popular mixed drink is ideal to serve
as an afternoon refresher.
Serve in a highball glass.

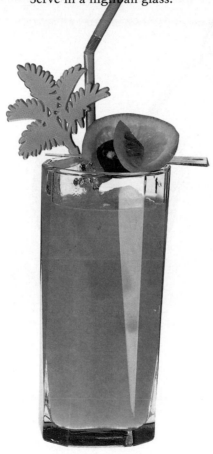

ice
45 mL vodka
orange juice
orange twist
maraschino cherry

Place ice in serving glass. Add vodka and top with orange juice. Garnish
with orange and cherry and serve with a straw.

HARVEY WALLBANGER

This long drink is a splendid way to see the afternoon away.
A dash of grenadine may also be added if desired.
Serve Harvey Wallbangers in a highball glass or large goblet.

ice
30 mL vodka
30 mL Galliano
orange juice
orange twist

Place ice in serving glass. Add vodka and Galliano and top with orange
juice. Garnish with orange twist and serve with a straw.

BLOODY MARY

This perennial favourite is ideal to serve mid-morning to enliven
and refresh. The first step is to mix the spices, sauces and lemon
juice; the vodka and tomato juice are then added. Vodka may be
replaced by white rum, gin or tequila if desired.
Bloody Marys are served in highball glasses. You can frost the glass
with celery salt (see page 61) and serve with a stick of crisp celery.

ice
dash Tabasco sauce
dash Worcestershire sauce
dash lemon juice
salt
pepper
60 mL vodka
tomato juice
celery stick

1 Place ice in serving glass. Add Tabasco and Worcestershire sauce, lemon
juice, salt and pepper; mix well.
2 Add vodka. Top with tomato juice and mix well; serve with celery stick.

BLACK RUSSIAN

Black Russians are very fashionable after-dinner cocktails.
Tia Maria can be substituted for Kahlua; cream can also be added
to the drink, making it a White Russian. For a long drink add cola.
Black Russians can be served in Old-Fashioned tumblers.

ice
45 mL vodka
15 mL Kahlua
maraschino cherry

Place ice in serving glass. Pour over vodka and Kahlua. Serve with a
maraschino cherry and a straw.

CHI CHI

Here is a tantalising cocktail to enjoy as an afternoon or evening
drink. Use unsweetened pineapple juice and good quality
coconut cream.
Serve your Chi Chi in a large goblet.

ice
45 mL vodka
15 mL Cointreau
30 mL coconut cream
120 mL pineapple juice
fresh pineapple slice
maraschino cherry

1 Place ice, vodka, Cointreau, coconut cream and pineapple juice in a
shaker; shake to mix.
2 Strain into serving glass and garnish with pineapple and cherry.

BLUE SPRING

This attractive cocktail is a splendid afternoon drink, ideal to serve
at poolside and garden parties.
Serve it in a highball glass.

ice
30 mL vodka
30 mL blue curaçao
15 mL white curaçao
lemonade
fresh pineapple slice
maraschino cherry

1 Place ice in serving glass. Pour over vodka, blue and white curaçao
and stir well.
2 Top with lemonade and garnish with pineapple and cherry.

MAI TAI

This delicious drink is a stylish afternoon cocktail to be slowly sipped and enjoyed. A dash of grenadine may be added for colour and sweetness. Amaretto is an almond-flavoured liqueur. If it is unavailable, use curaçao or another orange-flavoured liqueur. Mai Tais are best served in large goblets.

ice
60 mL light rum
30 mL dark rum
15 mL curaçao
15 mL Amaretto
15 mL lemon juice

15 mL sugar syrup
fresh pineapple slice
fresh lime slice
maraschino cherry
fresh mint

1 Place ice, rums, curaçao, Amaretto, lemon juice and sugar syrup in shaker; mix well.
2 Place extra ice in serving glass and strain Mai Tai into glass and garnish with pineapple, lime, cherry and mint.

ZOMBIE

This cocktail certainly packs a punch. If you enjoy rum it is sure to please. For a lighter drink use only half measures of rum.
Serve your Zombie in a highball glass.

ice
30 mL light rum
30 mL dark rum
30 mL overproof rum
15 mL apricot brandy
15 mL cherry brandy
60 mL orange juice
15 mL lime juice
fresh fruit to garnish

1 Place ice, rums, apricot brandy, cherry brandy, orange and lime juice in shaker; mix well.
2 Add extra ice to serving glass and strain Zombie into glass. Garnish with fresh fruit and serve with a straw.

PINA COLADA

This appealing drink will tempt those who like a creamy afternoon cocktail. For best results use an unsweetened pineapple juice. Pina Coladas are served in a highball glass or large goblet.

ice
45 mL light rum
30 mL coconut cream
15 mL cream
15 mL sugar syrup (see page 3)
pineapple juice
fresh pineapple slice
maraschino cherry

1 Place ice, rum, coconut cream, cream, sugar syrup and pineapple juice in shaker; shake well to mix.
2 Strain into serving glass and garnish with pineapple and cherry.

DAIQUIRI

Daiquiris are perfect pre-dinner drinks which should be made and enjoyed immediately. Some recipes contain a dash of beaten egg white to enhance the look of the cocktail. Egg white does not alter the flavour.
Daiquiris are served in traditional cocktail glasses.

ice
45 mL light rum
30 mL lime juice
15 mL sugar syrup (see page 3)
lime twist

1 Place ice, rum, lime juice and sugar syrup in shaker; shake well to mix.
2 Strain into a cocktail glass and garnish with lime.

FROZEN
STRAWBERRY DAIQUIRI

This version of the classic Daiquiri has become very fashionable.
You will need a blender for this cocktail. To make blending easier,
add the rum and liqueur to the blender before adding crushed ice.
Serve the frozen Daiquiri in a large goblet.

45 mL light rum
15 mL strawberry liqueur
15 mL lime juice
6 strawberries
crushed ice
extra strawberry

1 Place rum, liqueur, lime juice, strawberries and crushed ice in blender.
Blend until well mixed.
2 Pour the frozen Daiquiri into a serving glass and garnish with extra
strawberry. Serve with a short straw.

HOT BUTTERED RUM

Hot Buttered Rum is a splendid nightcap to indulge in on a cool evening. Take care when adding the boiling water to the serving glass; pour it over the back of a spoon to prevent glass breaking. Serve this drink in a large goblet or liqueur coffee mug.

1 teaspoon butter
1 teaspoon brown sugar
rum essence
cinnamon
45 mL dark rum
boiling water

1 Mix softened butter with brown sugar, essence and cinnamon until well combined.
2 Place butter in the serving glass and add rum. Pour in boiling water. Stir well to combine and serve immediately.

BETWEEN THE SHEETS

Here is a nightcap to let you drift off to a heavenly sleep.
Serve this drink in a cocktail glass.

ice
30 mL light rum
30 mL brandy
30 mL Cointreau
dash lemon juice
lime knot

1 Place ice, rum, brandy, Cointreau and lemon juice in shaker;
shake to mix well.
2 Strain into serving glass and garnish with lime knot.

BRANDY ALEXANDER

This delightful after-dinner drink is a favourite amongst all who relish a creamy cocktail. Use good quality brandy or Cognac for a superior result. Do not add too much nutmeg as a garnish– a light sprinkle is best.
Brandy Alexanders are served in cocktail glasses.

ice
30 mL brandy
30 mL crème de cacao
60 mL cream
grated nutmeg
strawberry

1 Place ice, brandy, crème de cacao and cream in shaker; shake well to mix.
2 Strain into serving glass and garnish with a light sprinkle of nutmeg and a strawberry.

SIDECAR

Here is a superb pre-dinner cocktail to please your guests. You can make this drink with equal quantities of spirit if you like a sweeter cocktail. Use fresh lemon juice.
Serve your Sidecar in a cocktail glass.

ice
30 mL brandy
20 mL Cointreau
25 mL lemon juice
knot of lemon peel

1 Place ice, brandy, Cointreau and lemon juice in shaker; shake well to mix.
2 Strain into serving glass and garnish with lemon peel.

BRANDY CRUSTA

There are many variations of this classic cocktail but this is our favourite. You will need to sugar-frost the rim of the serving glass (see page 60). Maraschino is a clear cherry-flavoured liqueur. If unavailable use sugar syrup. Gin, rum or whisky can replace brandy. Use freshly squeezed strained orange juice. Brandy Crustas are served in champagne saucers or cocktail glasses.

ice
30 mL brandy
15 mL maraschino liqueur
30 mL orange juice
dash Angostura Bitters
maraschino cherry

1 Place ice, brandy, maraschino, orange juice and bitters in shaker; shake well to mix.
2 Strain into serving glass and garnish with a cherry.

BRANDY, LIME AND SODA

This is a refreshing mixed drink for any time of the day. Use fresh
lime juice and a dash of lime cordial for best results.
Serve in an Old-Fashioned tumbler.

ice
30 mL brandy
15 mL lime juice
dash lime cordial
soda water
lime twist

Place ice in serving glass; pour over brandy, lime juice and cordial.
Top with soda water and garnish with lime.

B & B

B & B stands for Brandy and Benedictine. They are served together in a liqueur glass or a warmed brandy balloon to allow you to smell the heady aroma before you drink. It is a sensational nightcap.

30 mL brandy
30 mL Benedictine

Place brandy and Benedictine in a warmed brandy balloon.

MARGARITA

Margaritas are the most popular mixed drink using tequila, which
is the national drink of Mexico. This drink certainly has a 'kick'.
Traditionally the rim of the serving glass is frosted with salt
(see page 61).
Serve your Margarita in a cocktail glass.

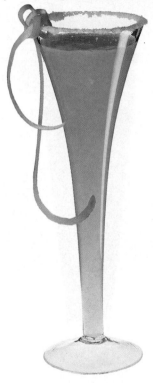

ice
45 mL tequila
30 mL lemon juice
15 mL Cointreau
dash beaten egg white
lemon peel

1 Place ice, tequila, lemon juice, Cointreau and egg white
in shaker; shake well to mix.
2 Strain into salt-frosted serving glass and garnish
with lemon peel.

TEQUILA SUNRISE

Another classic, this tequila cocktail can be enjoyed as a long afternoon drink. You may need practice at adding the grenadine to achieve the perfect 'sunrise'. The best way is to drop the grenadine quickly over the top of the drink so that it falls to the bottom of the glass and drifts slowly upward giving you a sunrise effect.

ice
60 mL tequila
orange juice
15 mL grenadine
orange slice

1 Place ice in serving glass. Pour over tequila and top with orange juice.
2 Drop grenadine into glass and garnish with orange slice and cherry; serve with a swizzle stick.

FRAPPÉ

Frappé liqueurs are served over crushed ice. They can be made from any liqueur or spirit or a combination of both. They are especially refreshing on hot balmy nights.
You can serve Frappé in large goblets or brandy balloons.

crushed ice
30 mL Parfait Amour
15 mL Cointreau

Fill a large goblet with crushed ice. Pour over Parfait Amour and Cointreau. Serve immediately with a short straw.

MELON SOUR

This pre-dinner drink uses a melon-flavoured liqueur. It is a deliciously *different* cocktail.
Serve your Melon Sour in a cocktail glass.

ice
60 mL melon liqueur
30 mL vodka
30 mL lime juice
dash egg white
dash sugar syrup (see page 3)
melon balls

1 Place ice, melon liqueur, vodka, lime juice, egg white and sugar syrup in shaker; shake well to mix.
2 Strain into serving glass and garnish with melon balls.

FLUFFY DUCK

This is the after-dinner variation of the ever popular Fluffy Duck.
It is rich and creamy as it uses advocaat, a Dutch liqueur made
from brandy, egg yolks and sugar
Serve the Fluffy Duck in a cocktail glass.

ice
30 mL light rum
30 mL advocaat
15 mL Cointreau
30 mL orange juice
30 mL cream
orange twist
maraschino cherry

1 Place ice, rum, advocaat, Cointreau, orange juice and cream
in shaker; shake well to mix.
2 Strain into serving glass and garnish with orange and cherry.

GRASSHOPPER

This firm favourite is ideal to serve as an after-dinner cocktail,
followed by strong dark coffee. Indulge your family and friends.
Grasshoppers are best served in champagne saucers
or cocktail glasses.

ice
45 mL green crème de menthe
30 mL white crème de cacao
60 mL cream
maraschino cherry

1 Place ice, crème de menthe, crème de cacao and cream in a shaker
Shake well to mix.
2 Strain into serving glass and garnish with a cherry.

GOLDEN DREAM

This cocktail uses two of the most popular liqueurs: Galliano, which is a golden liqueur with an aniseed flavour, and Cointreau, a colourless orange-flavoured liqueur.
Serve your Golden Dream in a cocktail glass.

ice
30 mL Galliano
20 mL Cointreau
20 mL orange juice
20 mL cream
maraschino cherry

1 Place ice, Galliano, Cointreau, orange juice and cream in shaker; shake well to mix.
2 Strain into serving glass and garnish with a cherry.

AMERICANO

Campari has a distinctive bitter-sweet taste. Infused with herbs and orange peel, it is served as an apéritif, often over ice, topped with soda. This mixed drink is long and cool and can be enjoyed any time of the day.
Serve the Americano in a highball glass.

ice
30 mL Campari
30 mL sweet vermouth
soda water
orange slice
lemon slice

1 Place ice in serving glass. Pour over Campari and vermouth and top with soda water.
2 Garnish with orange and lemon and serve with a swizzle stick.

PIMM'S

Pimm's No 1 has a gin base and Pimm's No 2 has a brandy base. Both are used to make long mixed drinks. Pimm's is enhanced by the garnish of fresh fruit and particularly a slice of cucumber skin which takes on the distinctive flavour of the Pimm's base. Pimm's is topped with equal quantities of lemonade and dry ginger. Serve your Pimm's in a highball glass.

ice
45 mL Pimm's
lemonade
dry ginger ale
slice cucumber skin
orange slice
lemon slice

1 Place ice in serving glass and add Pimm's; top with lemonade and dry ginger ale.
2 Garnish with cucumber, orange and lemon.

CHAMPAGNE COCKTAIL

Champagne cocktails are among the most agreeable drinks to enjoy at any time of the day. They are the perfect celebration drink and a great way to start an evening. Use good quality champagne and either brandy or Cognac.
Champagne cocktails are served in champagne flutes.

1 sugar cube
dash Angostura Bitters
15 mL brandy
chilled champagne

Place sugar cube in the glass. Add bitters and then brandy. Slowly top with champagne.

RITZ FIZZ

Another sparkling champagne cocktail sure to enliven the evening.
Use chilled champagne. Any liqueur can be used to flavour and
fortify champagne. Try crème de cassis, which is a blackcurrant-
flavoured liqueur, or Cointreau.
Serve the Ritz Fizz in a champagne flute.

dash blue curaçao
dash Amaretto
dash lemon juice
chilled champagne
rose petal

Place curaçao, Amaretto and lemon juice in a serving glass
and slowly top with champagne. Float a rose petal over champagne
to garnish.

B 52

This potent mixed drink is a heady nightcap to be sipped slowly. Grand Marnier can replace the Cointreau, making the drink a KGB.
Serve in an Old-Fashioned tumbler.

ice
30 mL Kahlua
30 mL Baileys Irish cream
30 mL Cointreau

Place ice in serving glass. Pour over Kahlua, then Irish cream and finally the Cointreau. Serve with a short straw.

SAN MARTIN

Here is a cocktail for all who enjoy sherry as a pre-dinner drink.
Fino is the driest and finest of the sherries. It can be served slightly
chilled as an apéritif or as the accompaniment to a light
first course.
Serve your San Martin in a cocktail glass.

ice
45 mL fino sherry
45 mL dry vermouth
30 mL gin
green olive

1 Place ice in shaker; add sherry, vermouth and gin.
Shake well to mix.
2 Strain into a serving glass and garnish with an olive.

EXTRA SPECIAL COFFEE

When there's a nip in the air that is the time to serve our Extra
Special Coffee. Use good quality, freshly made coffee.
You can either serve whipped cream separately or float it
on top of the coffee.
Serve your Extra Special Coffee in a liqueur coffee mug.

30 mL brandy
30 mL Tia Maria
15 mL Cointreau
strong black coffee
sugar to taste
whipped cream

1 Warm brandy, Tia Maria and Cointreau over a low heat until just warm.
Pour into serving mug.
2 Top with strong black coffee. Add sugar to taste and serve with
whipped cream.

MICKEY MOUSE

Here is a cocktail that both children and adults will love. Serve the Mickey Mouse in a highball glass.

ice
cola
1 scoop vanilla ice-cream
whipped cream
3 maraschino cherries

Place ice in serving glass. Add cola until two-thirds full and carefully add a scoop of ice-cream. Top with cream and garnish with cherries.

EGG NOG

Egg Nogs make a great start to the day. A good dash of brandy can be added if desired.
Serve Egg Nog in a large goblet or liqueur coffee mug.

ice
1 egg
1 teaspoon caster sugar
½ teaspoon vanilla essence
300 mL milk
cinnamon
maraschino cherry

1 Place ice in shaker and add egg, sugar, vanilla and milk.
Shake well to mix.
2 Strain into serving glass, sprinkle with cinnamon and
garnish with a cherry.

BOO BOO'S SPECIAL

This is a fruity, refreshing mixed drink to indulge in on a
long hot day.
Serve in a large goblet or a highball glass.

ice
90 mL pineapple juice
90 mL orange juice
15 mL lemon juice
good dash Angostura Bitters
dash grenadine
fresh tropical fruits

1 Place ice in shaker; add pineapple juice, orange juice, lemon juice, bitters
and grenadine. Shake well to mix.
2 Strain into serving glass and garnish with fruits. Serve with
a swizzle stick and straw.

SHIRLEY TEMPLE

Dry ginger ale can replace the lemonade and the cream if preferred
for this mocktail.
Serve your Shirley Temple in a highball glass.

ice
good dash grenadine
lemonade
30 mL cream
maraschino cherries

1 Place ice in serving glass, add grenadine and top with lemonade.
2 Use a teaspoon to help float the cream over the lemonade. Rest
the spoon on top of the drink and carefully pour the cream into
the bowl of the spoon. The cream will flow over it and onto
the surface of the lemonade.
3 Garnish with cherries and serve with a straw and a swizzle stick.

PIMM'S PUNCH

Have all the ingredients well chilled and add the orange juice and champagne just before serving time. Extra orange juice may be added for a lighter punch. Enough for 12-16 people, this punch may be served in highball glasses.

ice
375 mL Pimm's No 2
375 mL Southern Comfort
180 mL sweet vermouth
180 mL light rum
375 mL orange juice
1 bottle of champagne
fresh fruit
orange slices
lemon slices

1 Place ice in punch bowl. Add Pimm's, Southern Comfort, vermouth and rum; stir to mix.
2 Pour in orange juice and champagne. Add fresh fruits and orange and lemon slices. Serve immediately.

BRANDY ALEXANDER PUNCH

This punch is ideal to serve as a festive treat. It serves 12 people
easily. Make and serve immediately in cocktail glasses.

1 x 750 mL bottle brandy
375 mL crème de cacao
6 x 300 mL cartons thickened cream
ice
nutmeg
maraschino cherries

1 Place brandy, crème de cacao and cream in a large bowl; whisk until just
beginning to thicken.
2 Add ice to serving bowl and pour in cream mixture. Sprinkle with
nutmeg and garnish with cherries.

PINEAPPLE SHERRY PUNCH

This refreshing summertime punch is easy to make and inexpensive.
The sherry can be omitted if a non-alcoholic punch is preferred.
Use fresh pineapple if available. Add the dry ginger ale just before
serving. Enough for 12 people, this punch may be served
in punch cups.

375 mL dry sherry
1 ripe pineapple
300 mL orange juice
300 mL apple juice
1 cup cold black tea
500 mL dry ginger ale
2 passionfruit
lemon slices
cucumber slices

1 Peel pineapple, remove core, cut into small pieces and place in serving
bowl. Pour over sherry; cover and stand for 30 minutes
2 Add orange juice, apple juice and tea; stir to mix.
3 To serve, pour over dry ginger ale, add passionfruit pulp
and lemon and cucumber slices.

TOPPINGS

Toppings are those final flourishes which improve the appearance of a cocktail. They are very simple and quick.

1 *Grated nutmeg* is often added to creamy-based cocktails. Where possible use fresh nutmeg and simply grate over the top of the drink. Take care not to add too much as it could overpower the flavour of the drink.

2 *Chocolate* is a favourite topping for coffee-flavoured and creamy drinks. You can grate dark chocolate over the cocktail, or use a vegetable peeler for larger flakes. Commercial chocolate bars are also useful for this type of garnish.

ICE

The ice you use in cocktail making should be absolutely fresh. Cubed ice can be made easily and stored in plastic bags after freezing; it can also be crushed easily. Fancy moulds are available and are fun to use. Make sure that the fancy shapes are not too large for your cocktail glasses.

1. *To crush ice:* wrap the ice cubes in a clean tea towel and, using a mallet, hit the ice until it is broken into small pieces. A blender can also be used for this. Half-fill the blender with ice, add just enough water to cover ice, blend for 40 seconds. Drain away water and use ice immediately.

2. *To make flavoured or coloured ice cubes:* freeze fruit juices, soft drink, coffee, bitters or grenadine.

3. *To make decorated ice cubes:* add decorations to ice cube trays. Try strawberry halves, cherries, kiwi fruit, lemon or orange pieces. Half-fill the ice cube tray with water or juice, freeze until just set, top with garnish and cover with a little more water or juice. Experiment with different juice and fruit combinations.

FROSTING

Frosting a serving glass is a simple technique that enhances a cocktail and also adds a sweetness or a bite to your drink.

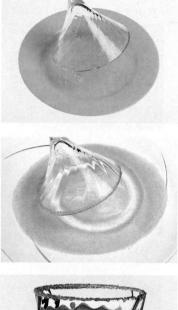

To sugar-frost your glass

1 Dip the rim of the glass in lightly beaten egg white until evenly coated.
2 Dip the glass in caster sugar and turn the glass slightly to allow the sugar to adhere to the rim of the glass. Do not push the glass too deeply into sugar or the result will be too heavy.
3 To achieve a coloured sugar rim, dip the rim of the glass in a small amount of grenadine, then gently dip the glass in caster sugar. The result will be a light pink frosting.

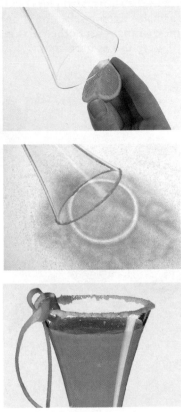

To salt-frost your glass

1 Hold your glass upside down and rub the rim of the glass
with a wedge of lime or lemon.
2 Dip the glass in coarse salt, turning the glass to allow the salt
to adhere.

HINT
You may also like to experiment with different frostings.
Try a mixture of ground coffee beans, nutmeg and cocoa. Tropical
cocktails will be enhanced by a frosting of freshly grated coconut.

GARNISHES

Garnishes for cocktails and mixed drinks need to be simple yet stimulating and appealing. They should not overpower the drink. Generally speaking, the longer refreshing style of drinks tend to have more garnish than the short, stronger cocktails that need only a simple or single garnish. Keep a selection of maraschino cherries, olives, lemons, limes, oranges and other seasonal fruits on hand to use as garnishes.

1 To make a *lemon or orange twist,* cut a thin slice crosswise and simply twist to serve on the side of the glass or in the drink. Try serving two different citrus fruit twists together.

2 To make a *spiral of citrus peel,* use a parer or vegetable peeler and cut away the skin, working in a circular motion. Take care not to cut into the bitter pith.

3 A *knot of peel* also adds zest to pre-dinner drinks. Use strips of peel and carefully tie each strip into a knot; use immediately.

4 *Melon balls* also make a delightful garnish. Use a melon baller and coloured melons to achieve a very different decoration.

5 *Pineapple slices or wedges* are used to garnish punches and long cool drinks. Leave the skin on the pineapple as this gives colour and texture. Use small pineapple leaves and cherries to enhance drink. Toothpicks will hold cherry and leaves together.

6 *Kiwi fruits, starfruits, bananas and other tropical fruits* can be sliced and dipped in lemon juice to be speared and served on the side of your cocktail.

7 *Strawberries* are ideal decorations for your drinks. Choose top quality berries that are firm, well-coloured and have a good green-leafed top. Make a small cut into the whole strawberry from the base to top to enable the strawberry to balance on the side of the glass. Strawberries can also be speared with a cocktail stick and placed over the rim of the glass.

INDEX